MONKEYS

LIVING WILD

Published by Creative Education
P.O. Box 227, Mankato, Minnesota 56002
Creative Education is an imprint of The Creative Company
www.thecreativecompany.us

Design and production by Mary Herrmann
Art direction by Rita Marshall
Printed by Corporate Graphics in the United States of America

Photographs by 123RF (Les Cunliffe, Eric Gevaert, Eric Isselee, Christine Sato, Nico Smit), Alamy (dbimages, Michael Doolittle, Edward Parker), Corbis (Tom Brakefield, GOPAL CHITRAKAR/Reuters, Gallo Images, Georges de Keerle/Sygma, Kevin Schafer), Dreamstime (Cbo, Chinamark, Ecophoto, Jangottwald, Ostill, Palangsi), Getty Images (Adrian Bailey/Aurora, Tim Graham, Koichi Kamoshida, Peter Macdiarmid, Michael K. Nichols/National Geographic, Renaud Visage, Joel Sartore/National Geographic), iStockphoto (David L Amsler, Mark Atkins, Henk Bentlage, John Carvalho, Ewan Chesser, David Ciemny, David Cloud, Darren Deans, Loretta Hostettler, Warwick Lister-Kaye, Jonathan Lyons, Yasmin Tajik, Simone van den Berg), Minden Pictures (Claus Meyer)

Library of Congress Cataloging-in-Publication Data
Gish, Melissa.
Monkeys / by Melissa Gish.
p. cm. — (Living wild)
Includes bibliographical references and index.
ISBN 978-1-58341-740-9
1. Monkeys—Juvenile literature. I. Title. II. Series.

QL737.P9G57 2009
599.8—dc22   2008009504

CPSIA: 020212 PO1534
9 8 7 6 5 4

☾ CREATIVE EDUCATION

MONKEYS

Melissa Gish

High in the warm canopy of the Amazon rainforest, the air is heavy with moisture. Pygmy marmosets

gather at the top of a massive acacia tree, its bark scarred by tiny tooth-gouges.

High in the warm **canopy** of the Amazon rainforest, the air is heavy with moisture. Pygmy marmosets gather at the top of a massive acacia tree, its bark scarred by tiny tooth-gouges. The marmosets lap up the sap that drips from the gouges. Tiny hands quickly seize leafhoppers and moths from the tips of leaves. Some marmosets climb slender vines to slurp nectar from luscious papayas. As a marmoset carefully grooms its mate, picking dust from

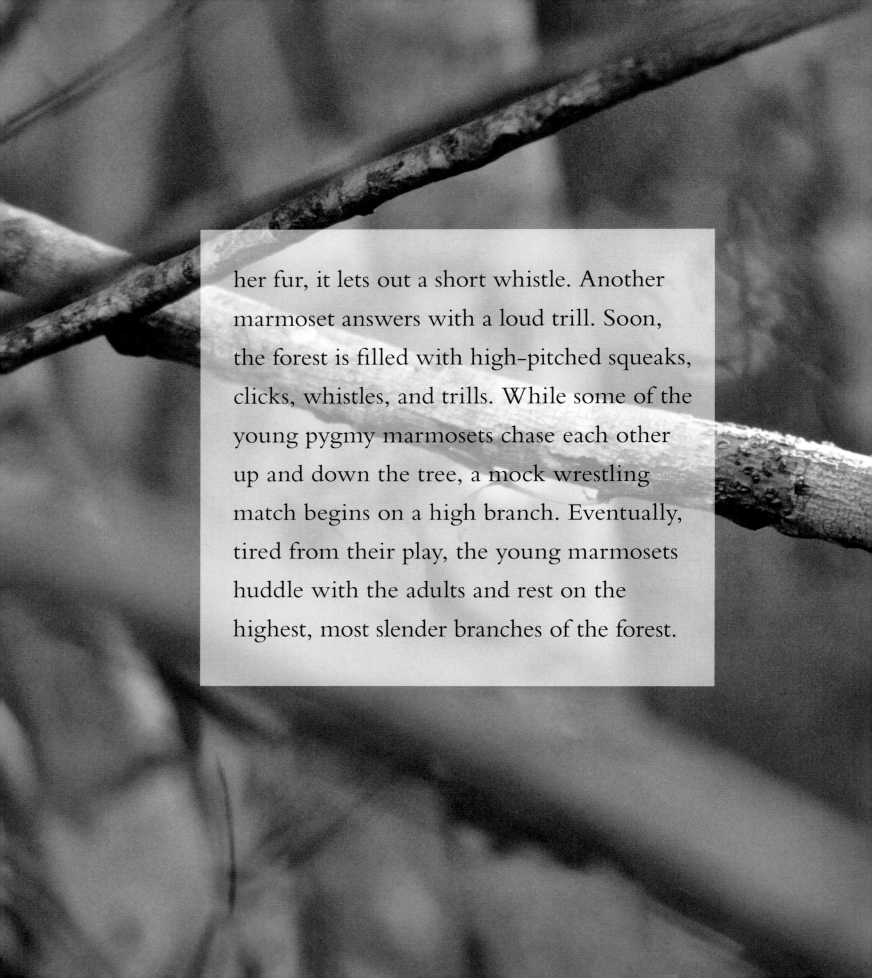

her fur, it lets out a short whistle. Another marmoset answers with a loud trill. Soon, the forest is filled with high-pitched squeaks, clicks, whistles, and trills. While some of the young pygmy marmosets chase each other up and down the tree, a mock wrestling match begins on a high branch. Eventually, tired from their play, the young marmosets huddle with the adults and rest on the highest, most slender branches of the forest.

WHERE IN THE WORLD THEY LIVE

EXAMPLES OF NEW WORLD MONKEYS

■ **Pygmy Marmoset**
rainforests of
northern South
America

□ **Titi**
South American
countries of
Colombia, Peru,
Brazil, and
Paraguay

■ **Capuchin**
Central and South
America

□ **Squirrel Monkey**
tropical forests
of Central and
South America

The nearly 200 species of monkey
are native to parts of five of Earth's
continents. Divided into Old World and
New World species, monkeys are most
common in Africa, South America,
and Asia, but some are found in the
southernmost region of North America
(Central America) and in parts of
southern Europe as well. No monkeys
are found in Australia or Antarctica.
The colored squares represent the
locations of eight examples of Old
World and New World monkeys.

EXAMPLES OF OLD WORLD MONKEYS

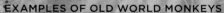

■ **Mandrill**
west-central
Africa, from
Nigeria to Congo

■ **Guenon**
sub-Saharan
Africa

■ **Chacma Baboon**
southern Africa

■ **Barbary Macaque**
North African
countries of Algeria
and Morocco,
and Gibraltar

TWO WORLDS OF MONKEYS

Colobus monkeys have tiny thumbs or none at all; their name comes from a Greek word meaning "cut short."

Monkeys are found almost everywhere on Earth. They belong to the group of mammals known as primates. There are six kinds of primates: lemurs, lorises, tarsiers, monkeys, apes, and humans. Of the more than 300 primate species in the world, about 200 of them are monkeys. Many species of baboons, guenons (*guh-NAWNS*), macaques (*muh-KAHKS*), marmosets, and tamarins are classified as monkeys.

All monkeys have slender bodies with long arms and legs. Most have five fingers on each hand and five toes on each foot, just like humans. Their fingers and thumbs give them a strong grip. Monkeys are sometimes confused with apes. While the two are related, they are very different from one another. Apes don't have tails, but all monkeys do (even though some are very short). Apes have flat noses, while monkeys have snouts. Monkeys are not as intelligent as apes, and most of them are smaller than apes. Additionally, apes are not found in North or South America or Europe, but monkeys—one of the most varied groups of all mammals—are found all over the world.

Another word for an elephant's trunk is "proboscis"; the proboscis monkey is named for its long, trunk-like nose.

Monkeys are divided into two groups: Old World and New World monkeys. Old World monkeys are native to Africa and Asia. New World monkeys are found in Mexico, Central America, and South America. Noses are a telling physical characteristic when it comes to distinguishing between Old and New World monkeys. Most Old World monkeys have small, curved nostrils set close together, while most New World monkeys have broad noses with round nostrils that are set far apart. Another physical difference is that New World monkeys do not have cheek pouches, but most Old World monkeys do, and they use them to store food that will be eaten later. Also, some Old World monkeys have hard, hairless pads on their rumps, but New World monkeys do not.

The **prehensile** tail is a remarkable feature of New World monkeys. The grip of a prehensile tail is so strong that a monkey can hang from a tree branch by its tail for a long time while feeding. Some monkeys' tails are so sensitive that they can be used to pluck a single leaf from a branch. Monkeys can also use their tails as a third hand to help them climb trees and swing from limb to limb more quickly.

The Old World spectacled langur, with the white rings around its eyes, is also known as the dusky leaf monkey.

Geladas are suited to higher altitudes and live at elevations of 4,600 to 14,000 feet (1,402–4,267 m).

Most monkeys prefer to live in rainforest or savanna climates. Only a few species can survive where the weather is cold. All New World and some Old World monkeys are arboreal, meaning they live primarily in trees. A few species, such as macaques and baboons, are suited for life on the ground. The gelada is the world's only grazing monkey, living on the grasslands of the African country of Ethiopia. The Japanese macaque is the northernmost monkey, and it is capable of living in more than three feet (.9 m) of snow in temperatures as low as 5 °F (-15 °C).

Scientists argue about the origins of New World monkeys. The most popular idea suggests that Old World monkeys emerged first and spread across Africa. About 35 million years ago, some of these monkeys accidentally traveled on huge, floating mats of vegetation across the Atlantic Ocean to South America. These monkeys then changed over time, developing different features that helped them adapt to their new surroundings. Today, the South American country of Brazil contains one-third of the world's monkey species.

Most monkeys are diurnal, meaning they are active during the daytime. Only one species is nocturnal, or

The only wild monkey in Europe is the tailless Barbary macaque, found in parts of northern Africa and the British territory of Gibraltar.

active at night. That is the South American douroucouli (*dor-uh-KOO-lee*), or owl monkey. Douroucoulis, like owls, have large, yellow-brown eyes, but that does not enable them to see better in the dark. These shy monkeys probably would not survive if they had to compete with more aggressive monkeys for food, so they have adapted to feeding at night, while all of the other monkeys in the forest are asleep.

The ability to see color also affects how monkeys find food. Since they feed in the dark, owl monkeys do not need to see colors. They are monochromatic and can see only shades of black. Most Old World monkeys are trichromatic. This means that they can see all three primary colors (blue, green, and red), so their vision is the same as humans'. Other monkeys are dichromatic and can see only two colors—blue and green. New World monkeys vary in their vision capabilities. Within various species of tamarins and spider monkeys, males are dichromatic, but females are trichromatic.

One of the world's largest and heaviest monkeys is the chacma baboon, also called the cape baboon. It can grow to be 47 inches (119 cm) tall and usually weighs

about 66 pounds (30 kg). Living in southern Africa's plains and parts of the Kalahari Desert, this baboon is a ground-dwelling species. In contrast to the baboon, South America's pygmy marmoset is the world's smallest monkey, measuring just six inches (15 cm) long. Its tail adds another nine inches (23 cm).

Female geladas may somewhat physically resemble young baboons, but geladas are not true baboons.

The Diana monkey was named for the Roman goddess of hunting because the stripe on its forehead resembles Diana's bow.

The more than 20 species of guenon are some of the most colorful monkeys in the world. The moustached monkey, for example, has a bright blue face with a white "moustache." All guenons are Old World monkeys that live throughout sub-Saharan Africa. Their close relative, the mandrill, is from tropical western Africa and has blue and scarlet markings on its face that grow darker as the monkey ages. Because the mandrill is very large—males can weigh up to 77 pounds (35 kg)—it is sometimes incorrectly called an ape.

Titis (*TEE-tees*) are New World monkeys with long, non-prehensile tails. Some species are marked with stripes on their necks or heads. While 28 species have been named, new ones are still being discovered deep in the Amazon rainforest. Smaller than titis, tamarins are among the smallest of the primates, measuring between six and nine inches (15–23 cm) long. Their tails can add another 9 to 13 inches (23–33 cm).

Capuchin monkeys, with their "caps" of hair, are named after 16th-century monks whose hooded robes they resemble. Capuchins are among the most intelligent of the New World monkeys and likely look the most like the earliest monkeys on Earth.

The white-headed capuchin is mostly black except for the white fur on the front of its body and face.

The Zanzibar red colobus is one of nine species of red colobus and is now considered to be endangered.

JUST HANGING OUT

When traveling through the treetops, the long-tailed macaque can leap distances of up to 17 feet (5 m).

M onkeys are long lived. Depending on the species, a monkey can live in the wild anywhere from 10 to 50 years. Some monkeys in captivity can live more than 40 years, thanks to proper health care and the nonexistence of predators.

Most monkeys have no specific breeding season and will breed with many partners. With few exceptions, females are fertile year-round. This is why many troops, or groups of monkeys, include offspring of different ages. Most monkeys are ready to be mothers by age five or seven. The process of choosing a mate varies by species. Toque macaque females, for example, are forced to breed only with the alpha male, or troop leader, or with males the alpha selects for the female. Female colobus monkeys, however, attract males by tongue smacking. If a female smacks her tongue at a male, she is telling him that he is an acceptable mate. Male woolly monkeys, on the other hand, shake tree branches to get the attention of a potential mate.

Four to eight months after monkeys have mated, the female gives birth. Most monkeys produce just one or

The ground-dwelling African patas monkey is the fastest primate on Earth. It can reach speeds of up to 35 miles (56 km) per hour.

two offspring at a time. Marmosets, however, almost always have twins—or sometimes triplets. For the first several months of its life, the young monkey will cling to its mother. Since mother monkeys produce milk for their babies, they must eat a lot, and carrying a baby makes foraging for food a slow business. Oftentimes, fathers or other members of the troop will carry the babies to give mothers a chance to hunt for food unburdened.

Depending on the species, monkeys reach maturity anywhere from age three to five. At that point, females will usually choose to stay with the troop, but males will often leave to join a neighboring family troop or gather with other young males to create a bachelor troop. Bachelor troops are usually small, but family troops vary in size, depending on the species of monkey. Titi troops, for example, may have only five members: two parents that have mated for life and three female offspring. Squirrel monkeys, on the other hand, may gather in troops of up to 100 individuals.

Ethiopian geladas form the largest monkey troops in the world, numbering from 350 to 650 individuals. These monkeys spend their days picking grass to eat, so they do

not have time to constantly groom each other. To maintain close relationships with one another, they "chatter" instead, making a variety of sounds to communicate from distances across a wide, grassy savanna.

Communication and membership in a troop are vital to a monkey's well-being. Monkeys and other primates are the most social of all mammals. They need to be with others of their kind for companionship and support. Living in a troop also makes it easier to find food and to take care of their young.

Of all monkeys, titis have the most complex system of vocal communication within their small family groups.

The nocturnal owl monkeys live in family groups consisting of a male and female and their immature offspring.

Several monkey troops of different species may live together in an area of the rainforest. They do this to help each other. Leaf-eating monkeys feeding in the trees look down and watch for predators such as jaguars. Smaller monkeys that feed higher up in the canopy look skyward, remaining watchful for birds of prey such as harpy eagles. Whenever a predator is spotted, all of the monkeys will sound an alarm by screaming, howling, or screeching. The calls identify the threat, be it a leopard on the ground, a **tayra** in the trees, or a crowned eagle in the sky. Even though the sounds may be different, monkeys can instantly interpret a specific call of danger.

Different kinds of monkeys communicate by different means. Some use vocalizations such as howling, and others use body gestures. One form of communication that is common to most species is social grooming. Monkeys will spend hours picking through each other's fur, eliminating dirt and **parasites**. This is a form of communication that nonverbally establishes **hierarchy** in the troop, serves as an apology during a disagreement, and strengthens friendships and family bonds.

Except for the owl monkey, all monkeys sleep in their family groups at night. Most species sleep 9 to 10 hours a night. They do not build nests, as their relatives the apes do. Arboreal monkeys simply huddle together in the crooks of tree branches and sleep sitting up. Ground-dwelling monkeys, such as baboons, sleep on cliffs or in the tops of palm trees.

Monkeys will usually share their food with one another. Most arboreal monkeys are frugivorous. This

Baboons have a "language" of more than 30 different sounds. They communicate through actions such as shrugging and lip smacking, too.

The mustached emperor tamarin is believed to have been named for German emperor Wilhelm II.

means that they eat mostly fruits and seeds. Part of their diet also consists of flowers and tender leaves, and some monkeys will eat honey if they can find it. Since all monkeys are opportunists, eating nearly anything if it's an easy meal, they sometimes will also eat insects, rodents, and birds' eggs, too.

The largest monkeys, the baboons, do not sit in treetops politely munching on leaves as many of their New World relatives do. Baboons are ground-dwelling omnivores—plants and meat are on their menu. Although their prey is small, baboons can be fierce hunters. They have been known to charge fearlessly at young gazelles and flamingoes. They will also work as a group to steal food from larger predators such as hyenas. Found throughout Africa, baboons are often hunted by lions, hyenas, leopards, wild dogs, and crocodiles. They protect themselves by living in a large troop.

The tiniest monkeys, marmosets, are gumivores, which means they eat the gum, or sap, of trees to supplement their diet of fruit, flowers, insects, lizards, and frogs. They are stealthy hunters, creeping slowly and silently over the thinnest branches to snatch living prey from leaves.

Because they are so lightweight, marmosets are the only monkeys capable of feeding in the very tops of trees.

Capuchins and spider monkeys are good problem solvers. They will look inside trees, beneath rocks and leaves, and under the ground for food that they believe is hidden. They will chase birds from nests to steal the eggs and dig up shellfish from muddy swamps. Their cleverness makes these monkeys particularly interesting to humans, who have used them to help unlock many scientific mysteries.

Sifakas are primates, but they belong to the lemur family and are only distantly related to monkeys.

MONKEY SEE, MONKEY DO

Monkeys have long been revered in many parts of the world, especially in India. The country's rainforests are home to many monkeys, and its native peoples developed special relationships with them over time. Even today, the Hindu monkey god Hanuman remains the symbol of devotion and service. He is one of the three major animal gods in the Hindu religion. A strong warrior who could run and fly very fast, Hanuman fought battles to protect people from evil. He could change his size at will, making himself small enough to sneak into places undetected and big enough to carry mountains on his back. In stories, Hanuman is described as having a red face, a golden body, and a long curling tail. His image fills temples and altars all across India.

Some religious scholars believe that hundreds of years ago, the stories of Hanuman traveled to China and gave rise to the tale of another mythical monkey: Sun Wukong, or the Monkey King. Believed to have helped the weak with kindness and to have battled the forces of evil, the Monkey King studied the **Tao**. He could

Found only in the Chinese province of Yunnan, the black snub-nosed monkey lives at the highest altitudes—near 15,000 feet (4,572 m)—of any primate.

A statue of the Hindu monkey god Hanuman (opposite) guards a temple in India, looking strong but prayerful.

Rhesus macaques, or rhesus monkeys, are captive-bred in their native country of Nepal and sold as research animals.

transform himself into 72 different things, from a tree, to a tiger, to a bird, to a mosquito. He moved across the sky by jumping on clouds.

In a sixteenth-century Chinese story called *Journey to the West*, the Monkey King is sent on a mission with a Buddhist monk and three other characters to retrieve a stolen treasure. Today, a Sun Wukong Festival is celebrated every year in China and Hong Kong.

Participants recreate the difficulties that the Monkey King and his companions faced on their journey by walking barefoot on hot coals and climbing ladders covered with knives. When it was announced that the 2008 Summer Olympics would be held in Bejing, China, thousands of people in that country asked for the Monkey King to be the official symbol of the 2008 Games.

The importance of monkeys to humans goes beyond symbolism, though, for monkeys are valued for their usefulness in science. For example, the United States relied heavily on monkeys—whose body structures are similar to humans'—in early experiments with space travel. The first monkey astronaut was a rhesus monkey named Albert. Sent into space in a V-2 rocket in 1948, Albert died during the mission, as did many animals in the pioneering days of space flight. But in 1959, the first monkeys made it into space and safely home again. They were Able, a rhesus monkey, and Baker, a squirrel monkey.

Two squirrel monkeys were occupants of Spacelab-3, carried on the space shuttle *Challenger*'s flight from April 29 through May 6 in 1985. The Russian space program

To plainly identify themselves, squirrel monkeys will smear food on their tails, much like how humans may wear name tags.

sent dozens of monkeys—all of them rhesus—into space between 1983 and 1997. In 1987, a satellite called Bion 8/Kosmos 1887 was launched, carrying a pair of monkeys named Yerosha and Dryoma. Animals are always strapped in tight for trips into space, but Yerosha wiggled free and was caught on video investigating his surroundings during the mission.

Daring astronaut monkeys are featured on the television show *Captain Simian and the Space Monkeys*. In this animated adventure, one of the National Aeronautics and Space Administration's (NASA) space monkeys, Charlie, accidentally leaves orbit and flies across space and time. He reaches a planet where he is given super intelligence and high-tech weapons in exchange for his promise to rid the universe of an evil enemy bent on destruction.

A capuchin monkey named Marcel captured the hearts of television viewers on the 1990s show *Friends*. The two females named Katie and Monkey who actually played Marcel also later appeared in many television commercials. More recently, monkeys have reached the big screen thanks to martial artist Jet Li, who played the Monkey King in the 2008 film *The Forbidden Kingdom*, a fantasy about a teenage boy's quest to rescue the imprisoned Monkey King.

Monkeys may have been revered in ancient Asian cities, found to be useful by scientists in many countries, and featured on television and in the movies, but many people in the rest of the world consider them pests and not worthy of consideration. This is plainly seen in the growth of the worldwide bushmeat trade. This is a business in which wild animals are hunted to be sold as food. With the demand for food in **impoverished** countries rising, monkeys are being relentlessly hunted.

Many animals hunted for bushmeat are protected by national and international laws, and the bushmeat trade is illegal in many regions of the world. However, **poachers** make so much money in this trade that they are willing to risk getting caught. But most poachers don't get caught. There simply are not enough park rangers to patrol all of the lands in which monkeys live. Even though the bushmeat trade is not a **sustainable** industry, neither hunters nor consumers are concerned about its future.

There are reasons for people to be alarmed by the success of the bushmeat trade, though, and one is that

Primates are used to study everything from space conditions to medications and surgical techniques.

The rare lion-tailed macaque of India is highly prized by collectors of illegal exotic pets.

most species of apes and monkeys being hunted for food are already endangered. In fact, one species of monkey, the Miss Waldron's red colobus, was declared to be likely extinct in 2000 due to overhunting.

In addition to hunting, such human activities as logging, agriculture, and the expansion of cities are having devastating effects on primate populations. Even in areas where some of the trees are left for wildlife, monkeys still become exposed to predators or often starve to death. Scientists have learned that, in a forest where humans have disturbed the trees and plantlife, harmful parasites are more common than in untouched forests. Many monkeys die from illnesses caused by these parasites.

The illegal pet trade industry is another threat to monkeys worldwide. While it is illegal in most parts of the world to own primate pets, many people still buy them. As long as people continue to buy illegal animals, poachers will continue to capture monkeys, often killing adults to steal their babies. Researchers predict that if the hunting, displacing, and capturing of apes and monkeys does not stop, 25 percent of the world's primate species will be extinct by 2018.

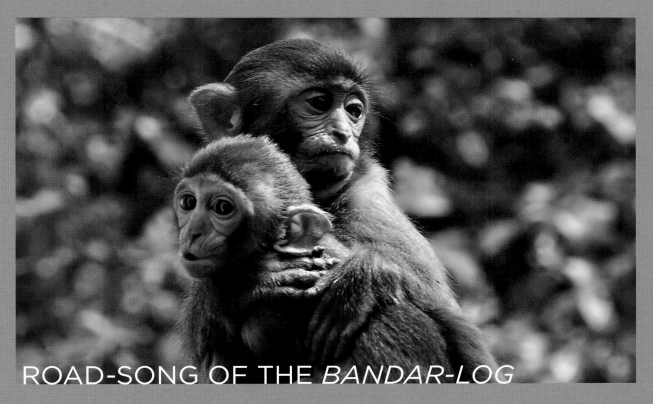

ROAD-SONG OF THE *BANDAR-LOG*

Here we go in a flung festoon,
Half-way up to the jealous moon!
Don't you envy our pranceful bands?
Don't you wish you had extra hands?
Wouldn't you like if your tails were—*so*—
Curved in the shape of a Cupid's bow?
    Now you're angry, but—never mind,
    Brother, thy tail hangs down behind!

Here we sit in a branchy row,
Thinking of beautiful things we know;
Dreaming of deeds that we mean to do,
All complete, in a minute or two—
Something noble and grand and good,
Won by merely wishing we could.
    Now we're going to—never mind,
    Brother, thy tail hangs down behind!

All the talk we ever have heard
Uttered by bat or beast or bird—
Hide or fin or scale or feather—
Jabber it quickly and all together!
Excellent! Wonderful! Once again!
Now we are talking just like men.
    Let's pretend we are . . . never mind,
    Brother, thy tail hangs down behind!
    This is the way of the Monkey-kind.

Then join our leaping lines that scumfish through the pines,
That rocket by where, light and high, the wild-grape swings.
By the rubbish in our wake, and the noble noise we make,
Be sure, be sure, we're going to do some splendid things!

Rudyard Kipling (1865–1936), from The Jungle Book

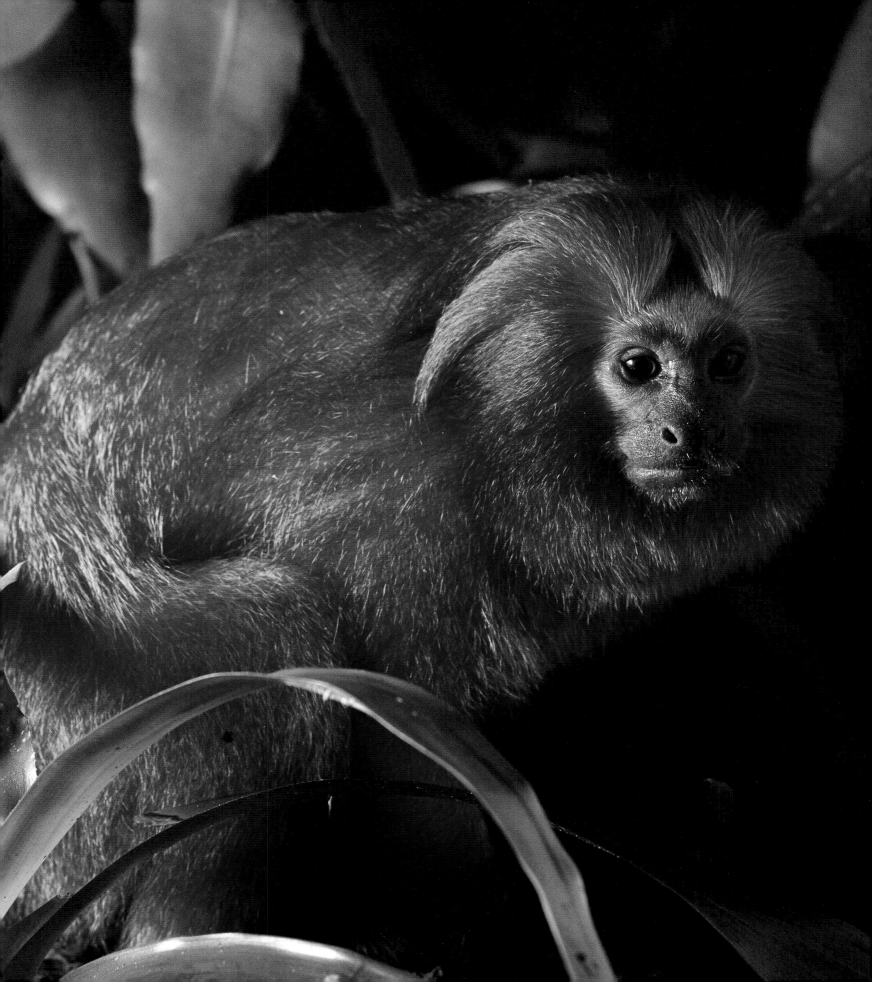

AN UNCERTAIN FUTURE

The best way to protect monkeys from extinction is to learn more about how they live and function in their **ecosystems**. Scientists around the world perform extensive research on everything from monkey origins and troop behaviors to feeding and breeding patterns. Studies about the ways that changing environments affect monkeys are also helpful in understanding the roles that human activity, natural predators, and weather play in the lives of monkeys.

Thousands of monkey fossils have been found in recent decades. They show how the environment played a role in the **evolution** of monkeys. In places where monkeys were once threatened by land predators, monkeys adapted to life in the trees, where they would be safer. In more deserted, treeless places, monkeys such as baboons changed into large ground-dwellers and developed sharp teeth and claws. With few predators capable of harming them, baboons moved up near the top of the **food chain**.

Fossils found in China suggest that the earliest monkey ancestor dates back to 45 million years ago. It was about

Due to the loss of trees in their native habitat, only about 1,500 golden lion tamarins (opposite) exist in the wild, living in a Brazilian game reserve.

The five-inch (12 cm) tarsier has characteristics similar to the earliest primates that evolved on Earth.

the size of a mouse and weighed just one ounce (28 g). One of the oldest fossils of a monkey skull more like today's monkeys was uncovered in Egypt in 1997. It is 15 million years old. Strong front teeth capable of biting through the hard rinds of fruit indicate that this monkey ate mostly fruit rather than leaves. Its skull can fit in the palm of a person's hand. Fossils of monkeys that lived just 100,000 years ago have been found in South America. These monkeys, called *Protopithecus*, were the shape of spider monkeys, with longer arms than legs, but they weighed twice as much as today's spider monkeys—about 50 pounds (23 kg).

Primate research helps not only monkeys but people as well. Learning about primates gives scientists insight into the workings of the human body. Because monkeys and apes are humans' closest relatives, they have been invaluable to medical research. If not for the tests done on monkeys, millions of people would have been struck down by polio—a disease that has been eliminated in most of the world. Current research that seeks cures for diseases such as cancer and **AIDS** still relies heavily on monkeys as test subjects. And thanks to **neuroscience**

research on monkeys, humans now have a valuable
understanding of how the brain functions.

Animal rights groups have long been concerned about
the use of monkeys in research, and many new laws
designed to make monkey research more humane have
been enacted recently. Each year, about 55,000 primates
are used as test animals in the U.S., and about 10,000

Spider monkeys are not as socially advanced as most other monkeys, seldom chattering or grooming each other.

are used in Great Britain. Japan uses millions of primates in its research. Despite advances in the treatment of test animals, many people believe that using intelligent primates for scientific research is **unethical** and should be stopped.

In addition to medical research and efforts to protect wild monkeys, researchers study captive monkeys to observe various behaviors. For example, studies on how rhesus monkeys communicate using sounds, facial expressions, and body gestures aid researchers in understanding how human infants communicate.

Also, while monkey social life is quite different from human social life, scientists believe that studying monkeys will help explain how humans learn from each other and how early humans might have developed their **culture**. For example, from 2000 to 2002, Brazilian researcher Dr. Antonio Moura conducted a study of capuchin monkeys in the Caatinga forest of northeastern Brazil. He observed the monkeys banging stones to scare off predators. When different monkeys were introduced to the test troop, the new monkeys watched the stone banging and soon began participating in the activity.

This may not seem like much for scientists to get excited about, but teaching and learning behaviors is a major part of developing a culture, and only humans do it so consistently. The capuchins of Caatinga are unique in their human-like behavior, as no other nonhuman primates exhibit this rock-banging skill. This proves that the behavior is not instinctive in monkeys; rather, it is a learned skill—just like the skills human children learn from their parents and other people.

Scientists have found that human interference may have an influence on monkey "culture." The Japanese macaque has been studied since the late 1940s. Researchers first lured the monkeys to them by offering them food. Sweet potatoes were handed out, but the macaques didn't like the taste of the dirt on the vegetables, so they washed the dirt off. Now, many generations of monkeys later, washing food has become a learned behavior. No other monkeys in the world are known to wash their food before eating it. Only the Japanese macaques exhibit this cultural behavior.

The world's tropical forests are natural laboratories where researchers study the effects of **global warming**

Japan draws tourists to the Jigokudani Valley to watch snow monkeys soak in hot mineral spring baths.

The DeBrazza's monkey is also known as the swamp monkey because it lives in flooded forests, swamps, and other watery places.

on the planet by observing monkeys. The animals' behaviors and actions can help scientists learn more about the impact that droughts, floods, and extreme weather have on the environment. For example, scientists in Africa found that as land in the DeBrazza's monkeys' habitat began to dry out, the monkeys traveled across open plains to a wetter habitat. These monkeys never travel far on the ground, so this discovery was surprising to scientists, suggesting that climate change is forcing wildlife to react in new ways.

Unlike the DeBrazza's monkey, other species are not as fortunate to find a new habitat when theirs is destroyed. In China, for example, as forestland is cleared to make way for roads, towns, and pastures, monkeys have nowhere to go. The Yunnan Golden Monkey Conservation Program is a major organization that works to protect China's Yunnan golden monkeys (also known as golden snub-nosed monkeys), which are some of the rarest monkeys on Earth.

Efforts at conserving monkey habitats and protecting monkeys from the threats of human activity are growing around the world, but the task is difficult. Despite the work

of dozens of conservation groups dedicated to saving these amazing animals, monkeys continue to perish. Breeding programs at zoos and conservation efforts in natural habitats are helpful projects, but widespread education is the key to ensuring a healthy future for all monkeys.

Like human parents, monkeys teach their young how to develop certain skills by demonstrating behaviors.

ANIMAL TALE:
THE MONKEY SPIRITS

For generations, the people of the African country of Ghana have respected and loved the monkey, which they view as a clever animal with a friendly and curious disposition. It is forbidden to harm monkeys there, and some species are even considered gods. The story of the Monkey Spirits shows how people can join together and live in harmony.

Two hundred years ago in the village of Boabeng, there lived a skillful hunter who never missed his target. But when a long drought settled on the land, many of the forest's animals left in search of water. The hunter was not able to shoot as many animals, and his family grew more and more hungry.

One day, while walking in the forest, the hunter encountered the powerful female spirit called Daworo and began talking to her about the problems caused by the drought. As he talked with Daworo, the hunter walked deeper into the forest. Suddenly, he came upon five monkeys gathered around a pot. Draped over the pot was a piece of brightly colored fabric. The hunter was so stunned that he asked Daworo what he should do. The spirit told him to treat the monkeys as his family. She instructed him to take the fabric home to Boabeng. He thought this advice was strange, but he obeyed. When he took the fabric, the monkeys followed him home.

As the weeks and months passed, the number of monkeys in Boabeng village increased. Every time monkeys were born, it rained a little. Soon the village was filled with monkeys, and it rained more and more—the drought was over! Then all the other animals

returned, and the hunter was able to feed his family better than he had ever fed them before. The entire village feasted and praised the monkeys for bringing the rain back to Boabeng.

Word of Daworo and the monkeys in Boabeng soon spread to the neighboring village of Fiema. A man there searched the forest for Daworo; he wanted to ask her for some monkeys for his village too. But Daworo never appeared to him. Instead, the equally powerful spirit Abodwo came to him. Abodwo agreed to ask Daworo to share the monkeys with the people of Fiema.

When Abodwo found Daworo, he was enchanted by her, and she was equally charmed by him. Abodwo asked Daworo for some monkeys. She readily agreed and gave him several, asking that he take them as his family. The great spirit Abodwo took the monkeys to Fiema and watched the village thrive as the monkeys multiplied. But Abodwo became lonely for Daworo and went back to the forest to seek her.

Since they looked over neighboring villages, Abodwo and Daworo decided to get married, and the monkeys became the symbol of their union. Just as marriage and family are considered sacred to the people of Ghana, so are the monkeys. The two villages joined, becoming Boabeng-Fiema, a special place where humans and monkeys lived in harmony as family.

To this day, monkeys are treated like family members in Boabeng-Fiema. The monkeys are protected from harm, and they walk freely through the streets. When a monkey dies in Boabeng-Fiema, it is given a funeral and buried just like a loved one.

GLOSSARY

AIDS – a disease that causes the failure of many body systems and weakens the body's ability to fight off illness

canopy – the topmost leafy branches of a forest

culture – the behaviors and characteristics of a particular group in a society that are similar and accepted as normal by that group

ecosystems – communities of organisms, plants, and animals that live together in an environment

evolution – the process of adapting to survive in a certain environment

food chain – a system in nature in which living things are dependent on each other for food

global warming – the gradual increase in Earth's temperature that causes changes in climates, or long-term weather conditions, around the world

hierarchy – a system in which people, animals, or things are ranked in importance one above another

impoverished – poor, or living in poverty

neuroscience – the study of how the body's nervous system and brain work

parasites – animals or plants that live on or inside another living thing (called a host) while giving nothing back to the host; some parasites cause disease or even death

poachers – people who hunt protected species of wild game and fish, even though doing so is against the law

prehensile – capable of grasping

sustainable – able to be renewed or kept functioning

Tao – a philosophy, or system of thought that originated in China in the 6th century B.C.

tayra – a burrowing, meat-eating animal related to the weasel; it lives in tropical forests from southern Mexico through South America

unethical – not agreeing with or not performing the actions and behaviors that are generally accepted by society

SELECTED BIBLIOGRAPHY

Flannery, Sean. "The Primata: Homepage." http://www.theprimata.com.

Hook, Patrick. *The World of Primates*. New York: Gramercy, 2000.

Live Science Staff Writers. "All About Monkeys." Live Science. http://www.livescience.com/monkeys.

Nowak, Ronald. *Walker's Primates of the World*. Baltimore: Johns Hopkins University Press, 1997.

Primate Conservation, Inc. "Homepage." Primate Conservation. http://www.primate.org.

Swinder, Daris. *Introduction to the Primates*. Seattle: University of Washington Press, 1998.

A pygmy marmoset weighs half an ounce (14 g) at birth and gains only about four more ounces (113 g) in its lifetime.

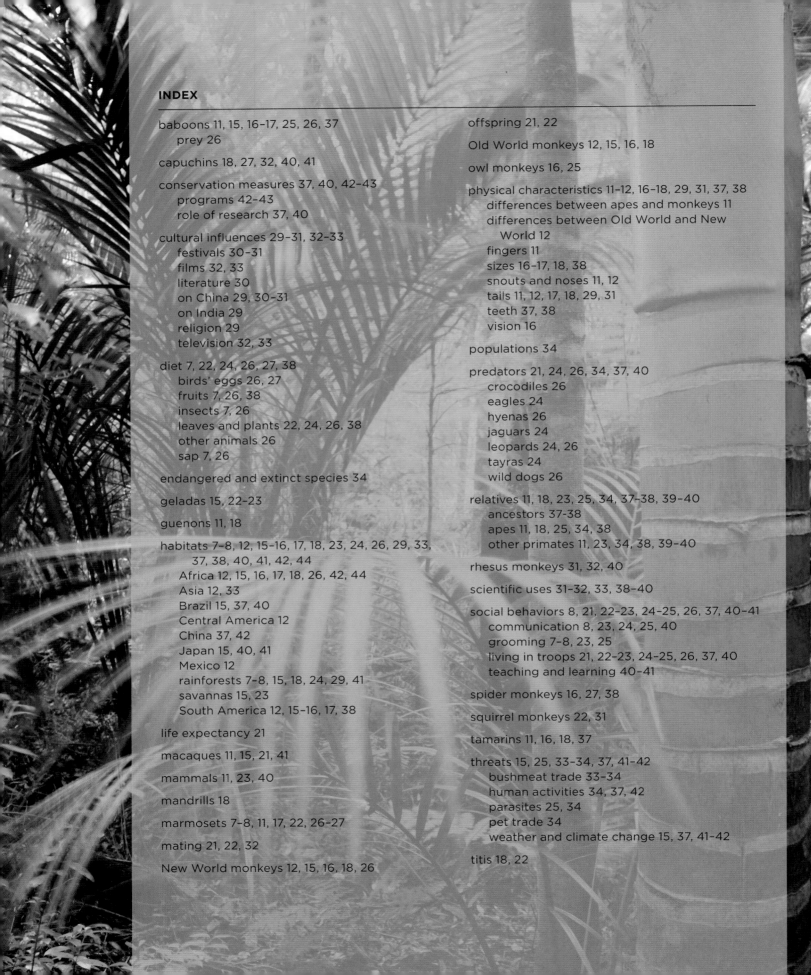

INDEX